The Forgotten Palaces of Calcutta

The Forgotten Palaces of Calcutta

Text and Photographs
by
Joanne Taylor

NIYOGI
BOOKS

Published by

NIYOGI BOOKS

Block D, Building No. 77,
Okhla Industrial Area, Phase-I,
New Delhi-110 020, INDIA
Tel: 91-11-26816301, 26818960
Email: niyogibooks@gmail.com
Website: www.niyogibooksindia.com

ISBN: 978-81-89738-78-5

Publication: 2006
1st reprint: 2007
Revised edition: 2011
Reprint: 2012
Reprint: 2018
Reprint: 2020
Reprint: 2023

Printed at: Niyogi Offset Pvt. Ltd., New Delhi, India

Contents

Colourful and ornate window of a mansion in Bagbazar, formerly an aristocratic area of Calcutta.

He, the Rajah of Amirpur, lived in retirement at Amirpur, dignified and aloof, bearing the landslide of adversities with courage. His palace in the city had been requisitioned as a government hospital for legislators, and the huge rambling house at the outskirts, with its ornamental gardens had been divided into building plots, and was the centre of the new colonies for refugees. The last occasion on which he had appeared in public was four years after Independence, when he welcomed the President of the Republic to a reception given in his honour by the taluqdars. *There were no illuminations, no champagne, no fireworks, no glitter of precious gems, orders, silks, brocades and ceremonial uniforms. This last reception of the* taluqdars *was a staid tea party, given by hosts who were soon to have their 'special class' and 'special privileges' abolished. Dusty portraits and marble statues of stately ex-presidents of their Associations, and of Imperial representatives, looked down with anachronistic grandeur on the tea tables bearing tea becoming tepid, cakes tasting stale, and the Indian savouries growing cold. Guests in Khaddar (loin cloth) outnumbered those in more formal attires. With grace and courtesy, Amirpur presided over this swan song of his order, while those who had habitually bowed before authority hovered round their gentle, dignified guests still hoping for manna from Heaven.*

- Attia Hosain, *Sunlight on a Broken Column.*

Preface

Looking at and photographing old houses has been a passion of mine for as long as I can remember. In addition to this is my ongoing love for India, beginning in 1971 with my first glimpse of the Taj Mahal by moonlight. This passion is due not only to my innate curiosity, but also the pleasure I feel when discovering an old mansion or a ruined palace. The mysteries that lie beyond a padlocked gate or an overgrown garden nourish my romantic tendencies. With photography I can record my discoveries, leading me to wonder further on the lives and histories of the families who manage to remain in such grand, evocative homes and the treasures they contain.

Imagine my joy in discovering the old area of North Calcutta, where heritage houses and history fill every crowded lane and secret courtyard. Languishing in another time and place, at the end of narrow lanes and behind untidy shop-fronts, Calcutta's rich heritage waits to be discovered.

A book like this is in part the result of visiting Indian houses, but finding and photographing these buildings is not all that is necessary. Historical information is needed, not just from libraries, but also from the homeowners themselves. I needed to make contact with owners and seek their permission to photograph. However, everywhere I was made to feel welcome, which invariably led to wonderful encounters with friendly, hospitable people, who generously shared their family history and allowed me to photograph their homes.

By focusing on a neglected phase of colonial history this volume will show another side of Calcutta. While much has been written and photographed on the city's British architecture and lifestyle, very little has been done by British or Indian writers on the indigenous equivalent.

By opening the doors to the homes of former rajahs and merchants we may imagine what life was like for a people who enjoyed British patronage and enormous wealth. Generations of colonial rule has resulted in an architectural style unique to Calcutta. I have endeavoured to highlight this hybrid architectural style of the Great Houses and their condition today, striving to exist in a city that seems oblivious to their fate. They are an important thread in the tapestry of Calcutta's history.

More practically, I have attempted to show a cross section of houses to exemplify the many and varied styles of architecture and the lifestyles that in some cases continue today.

Armed with a list of addresses, I sought out various sites, often to find that the house had long since collapsed. At other times I was led by well-meaning citizens to buildings they felt I should be looking for, often well-trodden tourist sites, shopping markets and even classical dancing schools.

At times it seems Calcutta 'found' me, especially when my photo documenting seemed to take on obsessional proportions. Whatever happened in the process, it seems very fitting and worthwhile that my interests and passions would result in a book focusing on part of India's important heritage, in particular the Great Houses of Calcutta.

Introduction

When asked to name one particular sight that sums up Calcutta, author Krishna Dutta answered: 'The decaying mansions of the Babus, who were the rich, British-influenced Indian gentry. They were built in a medley of architectural styles that V.S. Naipaul calls "Calcutta Corinthian" and are unique.'

The Great Houses of Calcutta are an important but forgotten part of India's architectural history. Despite descriptions like 'Bengal Baroque' and 'Rotten Rococo', these strange palaces and their heady mix of architectural styles seem to exist in an exuberant kind of harmony. Neo-classical, Islamic and Hindu elements can be found in both the structure and decoration of these heritage buildings. Ornate archways wide enough for an elephant to pass through lead to vast inner courtyards with temple-style family shrines. Colonnades catch the slightest breeze and cast shadows on marble floors, and above, latticed balconies derived from

An eclectic mix of marble statues line the verandah of the Roy home in Behala.

Pages 10-11: *The imposing Belgachia Villa of Prince Dwarkanath Tagore.*

Mughal times decorate women's quarters and co-exist with English painted glass, French doors and Venetian chandeliers. The founders of these 250 to 300-year-old mansions and palaces were landowners, merchants, intermediaries and cashiers for British leaders like Clive and Hastings. Others were moneylenders and tutors or interpreters for the British. They were all entrepreneurs who often held a variety of such roles. These men were indispensable to the British administration and this association was the basis of their accumulation of wealth.

With the British introduction of the Permanent Settlement Bill in 1793, they became even wealthier, buying up impoverished rural estates or zamindaris and employing managers to run them. Unlike the original zamindars, who lived in feudal style in their estates and were mostly seen by their peasants as firm but patriarchal figures, these new owners were absentee landlords, not obliged to set foot on their estates at all. Often their managers were cruel and unscrupulous, and the peasants suffered. For the wealthy merchants-turned-landowners, the countryside was far away and forgotten, and the pleasures of the growing metropolis of Calcutta beckoned.

Some of these urban rajahs had inherited titles, but most had titles bestowed on them by the British. Not only did this association with their rulers give them great wealth, it also gave them power, influence and status. Famous names among the Great Families include the Mullicks, Tagores, Dutts, Sens and Mitras. Although their fortunes have declined dramatically, many former aristocrats live in their ancestral homes in the historic area of North Calcutta. These decaying mansions and palaces are unique spaces of living history embodying tradition, culture and heritage that cannot be replaced.

To understand the history of the Great Houses, it is necessary to step back in time to 1690, the official birth year of Calcutta. Although Indian traders and weavers had settled in the area as early as the fifteenth century and the French and Dutch had set up trading posts upstream in Chandanagore and Chinsurah, it was the arrival of the British merchant, Job Charnock, that marked the birth of Calcutta. Dropping anchor on a marshy stretch of the Hooghly River, he laid the foundations for a British settlement on behalf of the East India Company and Britain's future imperial city was born.

At that time, Bengal was the wealthiest province in India and the perfect place for a trading station. The

Family portraits line the walls in the home of musician Sandeep Deb; a miniature Taj Mahal rests on the centre table.

Above: *Ornate doors and windows were the style of the day.*

Beautiful English-style verandah at the home of Partho Ghose.

area we now know as Calcutta was then made up of three village markets surrounded by jungles. Sutanati or 'thread market' was a densely populated and prosperous market of traders and weavers. Govindapur, the most southerly of the three villages, was a small, quiet fishing community and Kalikata was the least important, with very little recorded about it.

It is interesting to read Job Charnock's first impressions from the first volume of the Fort William factory records of 24 August 1690, describing the area we now know as Calcutta:

> This day at Sankraul ordered Capt. Brooke to come up with his vessel to Chutanutte where we arrived at about noon, but found ye place in a deplorable condition, nothing being left for our present accommodation and ye rains falling day and night. We are forced to take to boats which considering the season of the year is very unhealthy.

Despite these discouraging words, in just 100 years, Calcutta became known as the 'City of Palaces'.

The British first established their position by building a fort, approximately where the General Post Office is located, to the west of Dalhousie Square, now BBD Bagh. With little more than Company stores, warehouses and residences, it was not built to withstand an invasion. When the local ruler, Nawab Siraj-ud-daulah who ruled from Murshidabad, heard that the British traders were building a fort, he became anxious, which led to his troops storming the fort in 1757. The subsequent fighting destroyed not only the fort, but also the Governor's House and St. Anne's Church.

It was during this attack that the nawab ordered his men to incarcerate a number of British soldiers and civilians, including women, overnight in a small cell known as the 'Black Hole'. The overcrowding, high temperature and lack of water led to almost all of them perishing. Despite disputes over the details of what really happened and whether the nawab realised the cruel conditions on that fateful night, Calcutta has been burdened with the tragedy of this unfortunate incident ever since. The notorious Black Hole has become almost synonymous with the city itself.

Outraged by their defeat, the British retaliated later in the same year, when, led by Robert Clive, they defeated the nawab at Plassey. With this victory, the British in Calcutta began enjoying an atmosphere of great confidence. This period of optimism and economic growth marks the beginning of the rise of Calcutta's indigenous merchants. Their association with the British now gave them the opportunity to acquire great wealth and position. Soon the merchant families came to be known as the Great Families of Calcutta.

The new Fort William was built on the banks of the Hooghly River and the first phase was completed in

A busy street in North Calcutta.

ABOVE: *A sitar stucco atop the home of a music-loving family.*

1780, with a second phase of construction completed a century later. The construction of the Fort led to large-scale clearing of the area and the removal of any houses that could jeopardise security. In this way, the large grassy area of the Maidan was created. As more British arrived at Fort William, the Indian population were forced out. By 1757, the year that marks a period of consolidation for the East India Company, which began to function more as a colonial government and less as a trading concern, all Indians were evicted from their homes around Fort William. With the blessings of the British, and often with gifts of land to the most loyal, they moved to Sutanati. In this way, like many other colonial cities, Calcutta developed a 'White Town' and a 'Black Town'.

The city flourished and architecturally impressive buildings strengthened Britain's image of power. BBD Bagh became the administrative centre and classically elegant banks and hotels lined Chowringhee Road, now Jawaharlal Nehru Road. Calcutta was the City of Palaces, and artists like Balthazar Solvyns and the Daniells used the city as their subject, documenting the seemingly endless British buildings and streetscapes as the city evolved. In Sutanati, north of the city, however, Calcutta's entrepreneurial Indian traders, merchants and landowners were building their own mansions and palaces, and these went largely un-recorded.

Today Sutanati is simply called North Calcutta and is one of the most densely populated areas of the city. Here, off the ancient Chitpur Road, barefoot rickshaw wallahs compete with bright yellow Ambassador taxis to negotiate the labyrinth of busy streets and tiny lanes.

An opulent exotic living room in the Laha mansion.

LEFT: *Life-size Art Deco lamp in the dining room of the Laha family mansion.*

PAGES 16-17: *Colourful windows and columns of a Laha family home.*

This wonderfully chaotic area was once the playground of Calcutta's urban rajahs and their lavish entertainments, lifestyles and keenly contested rivalries are still evident in the architecture of their Great Houses.

This unique style of architecture began devoloping in the mid-eighteenth century. Wealthy, princely zamindars lived on sprawling country estates, where they ruled independently, had their own courts, tax collectors and even police forces, but as Calcutta developed, they began to build city palaces and mansions. Living away from their ancestral lands for long periods, they modelled their city palaces on their rural estates. Multiple inner courtyards, sprawling designs and Mughal and Hindu temple architecture reminded them of 'home', while they increased their fortunes in the new urban environment. These grand homes were not only residences, they were places of business and worship and the opulent lifestyles and entertainments that went on were conspicuous outward symbols of success.

By the late eighteenth century, wealthy Indian merchants sought to display their wealth and position in life by their association with their rulers. As the colonial city evolved, mansions and palaces in North Calcutta began to appear increasingly hybrid with the addition of more European influences. The Great Houses were modelled on the colonial forts, churches and homes being built in Calcutta's White Town. At the same time, the rural estates were neglected, becoming dilapidated or partitioned and were sold off

ultimately. The developing city offered a headier lifestyle for those with wealth and position.

The arrival of the nineteenth century saw great economic and social changes, which influenced the style, architecture and lifestyles of the Great Houses even further. A distinct European influence began to emerge and this new generation built even more extravagant mansions with their inherited wealth. Massive columns, pediments and decorative façades became commonplace, and many houses outwardly displayed the interests of the owner. Musical instruments in stucco could be found on the rooftop of a music lover, or female figures adorning a parapet would indicate the owner's love for dance and entertainment.

By the nineteenth century, many members of the Great Families became infamous for their extravagant and indolent lifestyles. They were intelligent, English-

A collection of Chinese, Japanese and English porcelain artefacts.

ABOVE LEFT: *Tiger skin decorates the staircase. Big game hunting was a sport of the landed gentry.*

Some residential mansions have been saved by being adapted for other uses, as wealthy merchant Loken Palit's home, now Science College, part of the University.

FACING PAGE: *An exotic painting of a mythological figure.*

educated and wasteful, and gave no consideration to the future. Calcutta abounds with stories and legends of these long-gone wealthy residents, most based on truth, and some embellished over the years. They form an interesting backdrop to an already interesting city. Their opulent lifestyles became known as 'Babu culture', a phenomenon exclusive to Calcutta.

The Babus had inherited their wealth from their ancestors and were determined to spend it. They filled their extensive homes with chandeliers from Venice, mirrors from Belgium, crystals from France and furniture, paintings, music boxes and dolls' houses from England.

Elaborate celebrations were held for the marriage of their pets and days were spent flying kites, while in the evenings, lavish entertainments were staged, which included bringing famous dancing (nautch) girls from as far away as Lucknow and Murshidadad. In addition, the Babus frequented the singing girls and *Baijee*s or courtesans of Boubazaar and the prostitute areas of Sonagachi. When they moved out of their mansions they displayed themselves in finery, wearing British-style clothing made in expensive Indian brocades and silks. Showy accessories included lace handkerchiefs and silver canes. They travelled in horse-drawn carriages or were carried about in palanquins. One Babu caused a sensation by using a pair of zebras to draw his carriage and at one time housing fourteen Rolls Royces in his Great House.

The opulent lifestyles of the Babus and the competitiveness with which they displayed their wealth became the stuff of legends. However, as the century progressed, their increasingly affected manners and wasteful lifestyles began to be mocked, not just by the indigenous residents of Calcutta but their British associates as well. Despite this, they continued to indulge themselves, caring little for discretion, preferring instead to be conspicuously extravagant.

Things changed when the British moved the capital from Calcutta to Delhi in 1911. Calcutta was no more the first city of India, the wealthy and influential Indian merchants and rulers were shocked and disappointed. No longer could they call themselves the Great Families. Suffering a loss of esteem and a decline in business, they began looking at ways to re-establish their influential positions and the blossoming Independence Movement seemed to be the answer. Political rallies and speeches became the newest entertainment in the courtyards of the Great Houses, and the most famous and influential thinkers of the country gathered at the expense of the wealthy merchants, some of whom now saw themselves as freedom fighters. The Babus of Calcutta were hanging

Exterior of a North Calcutta mansion.

Above: *Elegant living room of the Roys of Behala with Victorian decorative features.*

on to whatever they were left with and they chose independence from the very people who had enabled them to attain their wealth and positions.

The final outcome was bitter, however, as after Independence their situation changed even more dramatically. The British, who had given them power and wealth had gone, and ironically, many did not foresee how this would eventually affect their lives. The zamindari system was abolished, landed princes and gentry were forced to relinquish any independent powers and become part of a new India. Their vast estates were requisitioned or 'gifted' to the new government, and the compensation was neither sufficient to sustain their lavish lifestyles nor the large retinue of servants needed to maintain a Great House. It was the beginning of the end for a people who had no experience in dealing with everyday life. Not only did the Great Houses begin to decline, so did the area of North Calcutta.

In 1971, Prime Minister Indira Gandhi abolished the privy purses, and nationalised the mica and coal mines that many Great Families had invested in. This ruined many of the families overnight and heralded the terminal decline of the Great Houses. Nevertheless, the ancestral home remained, and many families found they could not agree on what should be done with it. Impossible to restore or maintain, they often resorted to simply drawing straws on who should remain and who could move to the cleaner, quieter areas of Calcutta. Some family disputes have dragged on in the courts for decades as the ancestral home decayed—one of the main reasons for the plight of many Great Houses today.

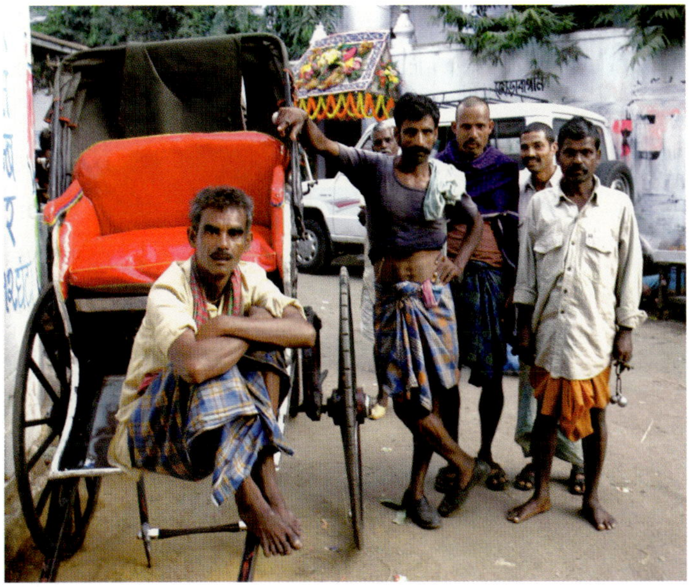

LEFT: *Rickshaw wallahs of Calcutta, near Belgachia Villa.*

RIGHT ABOVE: *The simple and elegant home of the Mookerjee family. Elephant tusks and antlers atop the fireplace immediately catch the visitor's eye.*

RIGHT BELOW: *Calcutta school children. Some great families have allowed schools to occupy parts of their enormous homes.*

Despite their predicament, many of the Great Families managed to survive. Younger generations acquired new occupations and skills, while they chose to live in just a few rooms of their large ancestral homes. These families have very little in common with their ancestors. Any power and influence they once had is gone and their homes, once built for exhibiting their extravagant lifestyle, are now liabilities. Land is sold off to developers and often the only thing left is the trust fund for the family deity. Where there was once respect, now there is more likely resentment or simply disregard.

In spite of this, there is cause for optimism in some cases. In 1919, the ancestors of Rajah Ramdulal Deb agreed to keep their 250-year-old ancestral home by forming a trust, which is maintained by the eldest son of each family. For this Great Family, continuity is important, and by keeping the original home, they retain their history and sense of identity. In other cases, families have leased or gifted space in their ancestral

An unusual covered courtyard. The Chatu Latu home. Fans take the place of open air.

ABOVE: *European-style outdoor dining in the home of Ashutosh and Mitali Laha.*

homes for much-needed schools. In some instances, the government has transformed a Great House into a hospital or a research institution. It would seem that in some cases, by transforming these enormous buildings and making practical use of them, there is some hope for their preservation.

After more than sixty years of Independence, Calcutta's history and heritage buildings are being looked at in new ways. During the 1980s and 1990s, particularly after the city's tercentenary and the fiftieth year of Independence, there emerged an increasing awareness, both locally and internationally, of conservation issues. Despite best intentions, the city's climate, which fosters a nagging dampness in brick buildings and insufficient funding, seems to have sealed the fate of North Calcutta's forgotten palaces. In some cases, family disputes have developed into long-standing court cases, eating into the inherited wealth while the ancestral home continues to decline. For many of these buildings it is already too late.

Magnificent ruined mansions now sit alongside small residences, temples, bazaars and hutments, abandoned by owners unable to maintain them or rented to tenants who know or care little for the building's history. To many they are hauntingly beautiful; to others they are an unwelcome reminder of India's colonial aspirations or embody feudal oppression. To some they are grand symbols of Bengali entrepreneurship and epitomise Calcutta's past opulence.

A ruined mansion on Nimtola Ghat Street; its rooms in such bad repair that even derelicts are afraid to enter. Part of the property now houses the Jorabagan Police Station.

Culture Dictates Form

Crowded Lanes and Secret Courtyards, Style and Construction

Few trained architects travelled to colonial cities during the eighteenth century. Instead, pattern books of architectural styles were used and adapted by military engineers for British buildings. The designs of Palladio were popular in Britain at the time and represented the power and permanence they felt they needed to rule India. This architectural style seemed ideal for the booming city of Calcutta. Through their association with the British, the city's rising merchant class had access to European taste and lifestyles. Soon British architectural styles, albeit in a hybrid form, began to find their way to the Great Houses in North Calcutta. Externally, massive pediments, extended colonnades and ornate capitals exemplified their style. The unrestrained use of European embellishments such as statues, decorations and cast iron railings now merged with Mughal and traditional Indian motifs.

Local masons were employed by the owners and given instructions as to the number of rooms required. However, it was often the head masons and munshis,

In private, a woman watches the courtyard below in the house of Motilal Sil.

ABOVE: *British architecture of the Raj Bhavan, Government House, Calcutta.*

PAGES 26–27: *Ornate windows in the upper floor of a Laha family mansion.*

who made the final decision on the style and decoration. As traders and craftsmen stayed in the same job all their lives, inheriting their professions from their parents and grandparents, the Great Families would deal only with their families' tradesmen who had worked for them for generations. This practice continued until when, after Independence, things changed and people moved from their traditional homes. By the mid-nineteenth century, Indian engineers and British construction companies like Burns Macintosh built Great Houses for the next generation of urban rajahs and wealthy merchants.

Cultural rules and lifestyles of the residents dictated design and form. Traditionally, a Great House consisted of an 'outer house' or the public areas, and an 'inner house' or the women's areas. Offices, waiting rooms and various sitting rooms were located downstairs. A servant would take visitors to one of these sitting rooms to wait, but if a female visited, a man could not receive her alone. The men and women of the family spent most of their days apart. The men would use the ground floor offices and courtyards during the day, going about their business, but never speaking to the women.

On the first floor were the public apartments, with attached verandahs opening inwards to the courtyard. These verandahs were generally long and narrow, and often featured a profusion of chandeliers, wall lights, hall tables and statues. The first level was also for the female members of the family and the children. On this floor, pretty fret-worked timber or wrought iron-laced verandah which opened inwards to the courtyards. Some houses had two or three sets of women's quarters, depending on the number of female family members. In these *zenana*s or women's

Ornamental crystal and enamel chandelier from Belgium, the Burdwan Palace.

LEFT: *Decorative floral motif on exterior walkways.*

quarters, the women and children would watch the comings and goings from latticed balconies, a design and custom derived from Mughal traditions.

The women and children were segregated from the men of the house during the day, only coming together at night in common sitting rooms usually on the third floor. Traditionally, women were expected to spend their entire time indoors. An old Sanskrit saying confirms this: 'A woman is someone the sun has not seen'. Even today, older ladies cover their heads if a man is visiting their home.

Both Calcutta's Black Town and White Town needed servants and tradespeople to run their enormous houses. The British built labour colonies in White Town, which were the beginning of today's *bustee*s or slum settlements. In North Calcutta, the Great Families had no reservations about servants living close by;

Left: *Indian and English decorative pieces on a verandah of the Roys of Behala.*

Below: *Hidden parts of a mansion - a view of the servants' stairways.*

Washing day at the Roys of Jorasanko.

Above: *Beautiful courtyard of the Roys of Behala.*

therefore, small dwellings were built inside the grounds or in hutments, which dotted the surrounding area haphazardly. Tradespeople like washer-folk, cooks, cleaners and oil pressers were needed, and to some extent, these servants, their castes and their traditional duties affected the design of the Great Houses.

Servants such as sweepers could only enter the house from the back, via special stairs, and then could only sweep the bathrooms. Cooks made meals but bearers were the only ones who could serve them. These many and varied servants accessed the houses through a complicated series of stairs and entrances and exits, which were invisible to the aristocratic residents. Despite their limited access to many areas of the house, it was often the servants, even more than some members of the family, who really knew the history and secrets of the Great Houses.

The grand entrance to the Roys' mansion at Behala.

The inside of these residences remained true to Indian cultural and religious traditions, while the exteriors were the result of British influence. Internally, the single most common feature of North Calcutta's Great Houses was the courtyard. In Calcutta's tropical, humid climate, cross ventilation was essential, and a courtyard open to the sky was designed for air to flow in, cross ventilating the surrounding rooms. Typical North Calcutta houses, large and small, are often called 'courtyard houses' for this reason. The largest houses had as many as three or even four courtyards of various sizes, each attached to the main building.

The early houses were seldom more than two stories, three sides of the ground floor consisting of storerooms, or quarters for servants, and the remaining fourth side, facing north, known as *thakur dalan*. This was always decorated with care, and on special evenings, such as Hindu festivals, particularly the Durga Puja festival, the whole courtyard would be covered and the area well lit, giving the space a magical, festive quality.

Generally, most old Indian houses consisted of a verandah on the south to capture the breeze, and faced east to the sunrise. Bedrooms had bathrooms attached, and at breakfast, the family would eat in the south-facing rooms. Students in the family were

English glass with Calcutta's famous green Venetian shutters in Laha Bari, Thanthania.

ABOVE: *Ceiling made of stone panels and steel beams, a type of architecture rarely seen today.*

expected to rise at dawn to study. The rooms were usually large, with high ceilings and enormous punkahs or ceiling fans made of fabric stretched over a light rectangular frame and operated by hand. Each room opened into one another through folding doors, with no intervening halls or lobbies. Other rooms opened on to hallways, which overlooked the courtyards.

During hot weather, the folding doors were seldom closed, instead a piece of cotton would be hung in the doorway, ending about six inches above the floor. This short curtain would catch the slightest breeze, cooling the darkened rooms and making the heat more bearable. On extra hot days, the fabric would be soaked in water to further cool the room. Despite helping to lower the temperature, these methods of ventilation did nothing for the privacy of the residents, furthering only the publicity of life in an Indian house. Members of the family always made sure they called out before entering a room.

Floors were covered with woven matting, again to help combat the heat. During the few weeks of Calcutta's cold season, fine Persian carpets or carpets from Mirzapore, would be thrown down. Many windows and doors reached the ground and were often French style. On the outside, Venetian shutters, usually painted green, would keep the rooms dark, cool and protected.

The ceilings were made of stone panels supported by steel beams, rarely seen today, as they are considered too expensive. Many roofs and ceilings were made of jaggery: a mixture of lime and straw, which was beaten repeatedly to make it waterproof. During British rule, only eunuchs were permitted to carry out this work. In

this way, a marginalised group was assured of a livelihood. Ceilings of later Great Houses were often painted in geometric designs and decorated with beautiful Belgium chandeliers in rich colours.

The British fondness for long impressive driveways and vast areas of land was not important to the Great Families. They were comfortable with having their family and their family-servants living close by and their inner courtyards gave them the required privacy. However, some Great Houses did have large grounds and

A classical garden statue in Laha mansion.

The thakur dalan *of the Roys of Jorasanko.*

gardens, with fountains and statues in the European style, while others were built on busy streets or in tiny lanes surrounded by buildings. Although much of this seems overcrowded due to the steady unplanned encroachment of the city, it is also due to the growth of their joint families. Over the generations, available land was bought and new houses built. In this way, a Great Family could own a number of different houses, of different styles and ages, which can now be found wedged into streets at different angles and aspects, clustered around the original ancestral home. These large joint families enjoyed living close together, and over time their multiple houses became connected by garden gates, tiny lanes and even suspended bridges.

The Great Houses with land and gardens often had two or more water tanks in the grounds. These tanks were more often like lakes and were enormous in size. The grounds also boasted accommodation for horse-drawn carriages, hand-held carriages or palanquins, where aristocrats would sit or lie for journeys and be carried by their servants. The Mullick's Marble Palace even included a zoo and stables for horses and elephants. Later, when elephants could no longer be kept in the city, their accommodation was converted to garages for luxury vehicles.

Former stables of the Mookherji home, now hold a vintage Rolls Royce.

Wealth and Competition, Urban Rajahs Set the Standard

Rajah Nabakrishna Deb (1733–97) has been called Calcutta's greatest zamindar and his palace in Shovabazar is thought to be the first and foremost in the list of North Calcutta's Great Houses.

Originally built by Sobharam Ghosh in the early eighteenth century, Nabakrishna came to own the property in 1757, with help from the British for his great loyalty. He had held two responsible posts early in his career, one as the munshi in Persian to Warren Hastings, the other as a political *bania* or intermediary for the East India Company.

The British awarded him the title of Rajah Bahadur for his efforts during the Battle of Plassey, when Nabakrishna convinced his peers to side with the British in toppling the nawab, Siraj-ud-daulah. Nabakrishna and others like him used their titles and awards to establish themselves as the founding fathers of Calcutta's Great Houses.

Nabakrishna was the most influential of the wealthy Bengalis who succeeded in creating a new urban culture.

The vast courtyard in Rajah Nabakrishna Deb's palace transformed into a venue for functions.

BELOW: *One of the two remaining brick pinnacles atop the* natmandir *of the palace of Rajah Nabakrishna Deb. Originally, there were nine, representing the nine jewels of the* navaratna *design.*

PAGES 38-39: *Interior of the* natmandir, *palace of Nabakrishna Deb.*

In some respects, this was due to the concentration of extremely wealthy people in a relatively small area. Competition was strong and this rivalry manifested itself through the architecture, lavish entertainment and extravagant lifestyles of the new rajahs.

After acquiring his new palace, he began a frantic series of alterations and renovations. With a huge labour force, the *thakur dalan* was completed in just three months, in time for a lavish Durga Puja festival to celebrate Robert Clive's victory at Plassey. It was one of the grandest and most memorable social gatherings in Calcutta's indigenous history and Nabakrishna set a new fashion that evening by inviting European dignitaries and entertaining lavishly. It was the first time British dignitaries were invited but it soon became a status symbol for the Great Families to invite European guests to attend their traditional Durga Puja ceremonies. Nabakrishna's position in North Calcutta society was such that other Durga Puja ceremonies could only begin after the firing of Nabakrishna's palace cannon.

Nabakrishna's love for entertaining was reported in the *Bengal Gazette*:

> Rajah Nabakrishna gave a nautch... in commemoration of Miss Wrangham's birthday. As the ladies arrived, they were conducted by the rajah through a grand suite of apartments into the *zenana*, where they were amused until the singing began. The surprising agility of the male dancers occasioned loud acclamations of applause. The principal female singers called nymphs and the swains to celebrate the festivities of the day with a few complimentary lines suitable to the occasion. After supper there was a ball, which was opened by Mr Livius and Miss Wrangham, who were dressed in the characters of Apollo and Daphne. When the minuets were ended, country dances struck up and continued till past three in the morning...

Nabakrishna's parties often culminated in a performance by famous dancing girls, brought to Calcutta from as far away as Agra. The Durga Puja, Kali Puja and Bengali New Year warranted elaborate dinners and parties, where Nabakrishna continued to delight in entertaining his English friends.

Interior of the ancient thakur dalan. *Painted terracotta plaques of Hindu gods line the whitewashed walls.*

LEFT: *Pretty wrought iron verandah, overseeing the* natmandir.

The original palace building features Mughal and medieval Bengali temple-style architecture. Some areas of Nabakrishna's palace show European influences, particularly the Palladian-style loggia at the entrance, the twin Ionic columns on either side and the British-style standing lions sitting atop. Nabakrishna's son or grandson probably added these features.

The palace covers a large area, but it is only once inside that the sheer scale of the courtyard, some 109 x 66 feet, can be appreciated. The whole courtyard has been whitewashed bright white with red and green trim, and the space is today rented out for meetings and cultural evenings. Sadly, on the other side of the palace walls, the stonework decays steadily and small hutments cling to the overgrown ruins. Here the restored *natmandir*, with pretty yellow and white interior, sits amongst cars and trucks, which litter the area, once a lovely garden.

Left: *An interior view of the magnificent* natmandir.

Right: *European cast iron lamps line the courtyard space of Nabakrishna's historic palace.*

Ruined exterior of Rajah Nabakrishna Deb's palace.

Rows of ornate European wrought-iron lamps line the grassy central area of the huge courtyard, which is surrounded by double-storied wings. Pairs of columns on the first floor create a verandah and support a balustraded parapet above. This is the first of the Great Houses to feature a double-storied hollow square design, rather than the traditional sprawling *mahal*s of the zamindari rural estates. At one time, the palace boasted a famous library of Bengali literature, long since gone.

The *thakur dalan*, at the end of the courtyard, is where religious ceremonies and social meetings were held. Piers support the roof with tapered shafts topped with decorative floral motifs. It is the kind of decorative style found in Mughal and Bengali temple

Classical columns of the natmandir*, the garden now used as a parking area.*

architecture. The wooden gallery inside is of indigenous style, with terracotta plaques of painted Hindu gods decorating the walls. Some are original, while others have been destroyed over the centuries and replaced with reproductions.

Legend has it that Rajah Nabakrishna Deb married six times and built a palace for each wife. Today, some seventy or more of his ancestors still live in various mansions, houses and small rooms on the street that bears his name. On quiet evenings, one can almost imagine the music and laughter that accompanied the lavish Durga Pujas, Kali Pujas and Bengali New Year celebrations that Nabakrishna and his guests so enjoyed!

The Spirit of a Great House

The Home of the Tagores

After nine in the evening, my lessons with Aghor Babu over, I am retiring within for the night. A murky flickering lamp is hanging in the long Venetian-screened corridor leading from the outer to the inner apartments. At its end this passage turns into a flight of four or five steps, to which the light does not reach, and down which I pass into the galleries running round the first inner quadrangle.

A shaft of moonlight slants from the eastern sky into the western angle of these verandahs, leaving the rest in darkness.

In this patch of light the maids have gathered and are sitting on the floor close together, with legs outstretched, rolling cotton waste into lamp-wicks and chatting in undertones of their village homes. Many such pictures are indelibly printed in my memory... .

With my face to the wall I gaze at the black and white patches, made by the plaster of the walls fallen off here and there, showing faintly in the dim light; out of these I conjure up many a fantastic image as I drop off to sleep.

Rabindranath Tagore, 1917.

The house of the Tagores in North Calcutta.

PAGES 46-47: *Sprawling gardens leading to the Tagore mansion.*

Rather than a forgotten palace, the home of the Tagores in Jorasanko is one of Calcutta's most important buildings. Despite its significance as the birthplace of Rabindranath Tagore and its transformation into a museum, the history of the house is firmly embedded in the mercantile and zamindari past of the city.

The first home of the Tagores was in Govindapore, but with the building of a new Fort William they were displaced in 1757. Jayram Tagore then acquired land in Pathuriaghata, North Calcutta, and built a large family home on the banks of the Hooghly River.

Jayram had four sons, but Nilmoni and Darpanarayan were the most successful. Nilmoni secured a job with the East India Company in Cuttack, while Darpanarayan stayed in Calcutta and amassed a large fortune through banking and business pursuits. When Nilmoni retired and returned to the family home, a dispute erupted between the brothers over the sharing of the property. The dispute was resolved when Nilmoni was paid for his share, enabling him to establish his own home in 1784, the first building on the Jorasanko site. In this way, he established a new branch of the Tagore family.

Though Nilmoni founded the original house, it was his grandson Dwarkanath who set in motion the rise and wealth of the Tagores, which gave the building its fame. Dwarkanath was born in 1794, and from an early age was groomed to become a great merchant with a life of close contact with the British. He was tutored in Arabic and Persian, as well as English to prepare him for a career with the East India Company and dealings with other English merchants. This background led to his work as an agent with Mackintosh and Company, then later as an independent merchant which included giving

Above (Both) and Left: *The Belgachia Villa of Prince Dwarkanath Tagore.*

The upper-level verandah overlooking an inner courtyard.

legal and business advice to other rising merchants and landowners.

Dwarkanath's quick rise included taking the position of dewan with the East India Company and founding the Union Bank. This was so successful that he managed to buy a number of zamindaris in North Bengal. Like many other merchants, Dwarkanath's acquisition of land led to the amassing of the family's great fortune.

When he decided to leave the East India Company to concentrate on his private enterprises, he was so well established that his success continued to rise. As a partner in Carr, Tagore and Co., he expanded into shipping and it was said his clipper ships sailed 'as far east as Canton, and as far west as London'.

Dwarkanath made extensions to the original home in Jorasanko, in particular a separate building that became known as the *baithakkhana*. At that time, the three-storeyed-building stood where the lawn is today, and featured arches and double columns with shutters and ornate cast-iron-verandahs. Dwarkanath used the building to stage grand parties and social events. Like Rajah Nabakrishna and other wealthy merchants, he enjoyed luxury and his guests included both Indian and English dignitaries.

His love of grand entertaining and opulence is particularly embodied in his garden house, the Belgachia Villa, where he enjoyed huge banquets and entertainments with his closest friends. Many great merchants kept garden houses, for pleasure and entertaining, apart from their family residences.

Along with social and business interests, Dwarkanath's most important and enduring achievements were in the areas of charity and social reform. With his friend

Rammohun Roy, he was involved in the abolition of sati, the founding of the Hindu College, which encouraged English education, and the financing of the Calcutta Medical College. With his philanthropic pursuits, the name 'Tagore' gained respect and fame in India and abroad.

'Prince' Dwarkanath Tagore travelled to London on his own ship, *The India*, and dined with Queen Victoria. The French king, Louis-Philippe, also received him, yet despite this great success and his enormous wealth, nothing could save him or other wealthy families from the business recession of the 1840s. Then, on his second trip to England in 1845, Dwarkanath fell ill and died, aged just fifty-two.

His sudden death and the subsequent drop in business took a toll on the family. Dwarkanath's son, Debendranath, now the head of the family, spent much of his life making the family solvent. The house at Jorasanko remained despite these tribulations, but gone was the opulent Babu way of life, and of entertaining on a lavish scale. Debendranath now led the family on a new path, that of spirituality. With his early association with Rammohan Roy, he joined the Brahmo Samaj, the religious movement founded by Roy in 1828. It differed from Hinduism as it was opposed to idol worship and the caste system and had at its central core the idea of one omniscient god. The Brahmo Samaj played a significant role in what became known as the Bengal Renaissance and though it was born in Calcutta it became known throughout India.

The family produced many illustrious, creative thinkers who excelled in life and who it would seem, prepared the ground for the legendary Rabindranath

Bust of Maharshi Debendranath Tagore, father of Rabindranath Tagore, at the entrance to the inner courtyard.

Tagore. Born on 9 May 1861, in the birthing room of the 'Thakur Bari', as it is known, he grew to be a Nobel Laureate, a leading light of the Brahmo Samaj and the leader of Bengal's social and cultural life for over fifty years.

As an eight-year-old, Rabindranath had already begun writing poetry. By the time he was sixteen his poems had been published and he was writing short stories and plays. Such were his talents that they cannot be easily classified, for he was an artist and a prolific and successful producer of poems, songs, stories, dance-dramas and sketches. His revered novels and compositions were so unique they influenced the style of Bengali literature and music.

The house in Jorasanko certainly played an important role in nurturing him as a child and the atmosphere of the home and the experiences and qualities he absorbed there surely led to his greatness. He recalled his family home many times in his memoirs, and as he and his siblings were mainly educated at home he wrote: 'We learnt much more at home than we had to at school'. He travelled extensively to all parts of the world, as within India, meeting eminent men of his time, including Gandhi. This meeting may have been instrumental in his eventual disillusionment with British rule and his move towards the Indian Independence Movement.

Compared to other houses of its kind, the House of the Tagores is not architecturally unique, but its history and the family that lived there have created a spiritual quality that sets it apart. The park-like gardens seem to encourage learning and quiet contemplation and the building and spirit of the place embodies all that is admirable in Bengali culture, learning, tradition and enlightenment.

Throughout his life Rabindranath suffered terrible family losses, and was saddened over Bengal's decline, yet he wrote of his family and their home with great affection. Despite his travels he returned again and again to the house in Jorasanko. The last time he returned he was to die there, safe at home and in the place that held so many fond memories.

Today, a large bust of Rabindranath occupies a special place in the garden and the home of Tagores is frequented by visitors and students alike who seek to gain a better understanding of the great man, his family and their contribution to India's culture. On the left of the entrance lies the Vichitra Hall, built in 1887, where Rabindranath held cultural evenings on the first floor. In this historic space, he would meet his admirers, hold literary discussions and recitations, give advice to young writers and hold live performances, such as the 1917 staging of his play, *The Post Office*. The gatherings became known as the 'Vichitra Club'. Today, the hall's corridor is used to display first editions of Rabindranath's books, the family tree and other collections and photographs of the Tagore family.

It is still possible to see the birthing room, the various living areas, the central courtyard where he performed his dramas, and movingly, even the room where he spent his last days. In this way, the spirit of Rabindranath Tagore lives on in one of the Great Houses of Calcutta. Rabindranath won the Nobel Prize for Literature in 1913. He died in 1941.

The bust of Tagore in the garden of Thakur Bari, a fountainhead of artistic inspiration.

Maintaining the Past

Marble, Mirrors and a Rubens: The Palace of the Mullick Family

The Mullick family, like the Tagores, is a famous name in the history of Calcutta and an important part of the mercantile and cultural fabric of the city. Unlike the Tagores, however, they were not zamindars, but gold merchants. The founder of their Great House, the Marble Palace, was Rajendra Mullick, whose father died when he was three. His mother Hiranmoyee Dasee and an English guardian Sir James Weir Hogg brought him up to become one of Calcutta's most famous citizens.

He received the title of Rai Bahadur for his efforts during the 1865-66 Bengal Famine, and was given the title of rajah by Lord Lytton in 1878 in acknowledgment of his 'charitable disposition and philanthropic deeds', receiving a large diamond ring as a ceremonial gift. His extraordinary Marble Palace embodies his great interest in natural history and both Eastern and Western art and culture.

This Great House is still home to members of the Mullick family who also maintain it as a private museum. It is the most famous of Calcutta's Great Houses, not

ABOVE: *An unlikely setting for the imposing Marble Palace on Muktaram Babu street.*

PAGES 54-55: *Massive and opulent, the Marble Palace from the garden.*

merely for its accessibility but for the opulent style and eclectic mix of art and treasures it houses. On a visit, Viceroy Lord Minto was so astonished with the ninety varieties of patterned imported marble on the floors, wall panels and tabletops that he called it the Marble Palace, and the title has remained to this day.

The Mullick family built numerous palaces and mansions in North Calcutta, including the Clock House on Chitpur Road, so named by Calcutta residents for the large Cooke and Kelvey clock, which sits atop its Corinthian columns.

Rajendra Nath Mullick was just sixteen-year-old in 1835 when he built this Great House, and it took 500 Indian and foreign artisans over five years to complete. Built in European classical style and closely resembling London's Burlington House, the Marble Palace is situated in the tiny lane of Muktaram Babu Street. Ornate gates flanked by guards holding tall iron spears go unnoticed by passersby going about their daily business. Rickshaw wallahs weave expertly through the crowds, calling out loudly to clear the way. Traders in silver sit in glittering showrooms and colourful sari shops are located beside small street-side stalls and tiny houses, their doorways a simple strip of fabric. Children play cricket with planks of wood and crowds surround the many cooking carts selling hot Bengali snacks. Amid this chaos, the enormous white façade of the Marble Palace seems strangely incongruous, with its driveway encircling an elaborate fountain and statues of lions, the Buddha, Jesus and various Hindu gods dotting the overgrown gardens.

The exterior of the palace features elaborate Rococo stucco work, and a portico with six Tuscan columns. It is impressive, with fourteen Corinthian-style columns on the ground floor and a further fourteen on the first floor, each separated by Venetian shutters. The house is topped with an ornately carved pediment. In accordance with Mullick family tradition, the architect was French.

Altogether, the compound consists of two separate buildings each with a central courtyard. The first building, which faces Muktaram Babu Street, was designed purely for the public display of the family's great and diverse art collection. The *mandap* is not used for pujas as it faces west rather than south, however, the family deity, an image of Jagannath, does reside for a few days every year, in a small separate temple in the gardens of the palace.

The gardens of the Marble Palace are Baroque in style and extensive. Ornamental stone seats are placed amongst groups of tall palms and tropical plants. The garden once housed a menagerie of animals and birds, Calcutta's first zoo. These days it is reduced to a

A guard with spear at the gates to the Marble Palace.

Above: *Doric style columns and iron gates herald the impressive entrance to the Mullick family's extraordinary Marble Palace on Muktaram Babu Street.*

The Marble Palace, Muktaram Babu Street.

ABOVE: *The billiard hall, fading grandeur, ornate plaster walls and a profusion of decorations.*

small, rather run-down enclosure, housing a collection of birds. In these grounds, a granite temple houses the deity and the Mullick family's priests. There are thousands of Mullick family members throughout the city of Calcutta.

The first room the visitor encounters is the elaborate billiard room dotted with statues and enormous carved side-tables. The walls are decorated with ornate stucco mouldings and hung with paintings. Other rooms follow, each as sumptuous as the last. Light filters through the shuttered windows adding to the atmosphere of faded Baroque grandeur. The family's fortunes enabled Rajendra Mullick to indulge in amassing a vast collection of art and artefacts for the palace.

Enormous glass chandeliers hang from the ceiling, their reflection multiplied in the floor-to-ceiling Venetian mirrors. Tables are crowded with Sevres vases, Bohemian goblets and Dresden figurines. Silent French ormolu clocks line the walls alongside swords from Toledo. Among the huge collection of oil paintings are a Rubens: 'The Marriage of St. Catherine' and a Joshua Reynolds 'The Infant Hercules Strangling the Serpent'. Each room is filled with the decorative, the ornamental and the monumental. There are so many artefacts - some are housed outside, on the colonnaded verandahs.

The blue and white painted courtyard is filled with statues, potted palms and a fountain. The altar is ornate with stucco mouldings, and strangely, Greek and Roman statues happily exist alongside figures from the Hindu scriptures in the *thakur dalan*.

The second building lies parallel to the first. The ground floor consists of a kitchen, servants' rooms, a large dining room and storage rooms. Functional in design, the upper floor also has a family residence, with a shrine for private worship.

Despite their wealth or perhaps because of it, the family have maintained a long tradition of caring for the needy. Rajendra's father, Nilmoni Mullick was a philanthropist, who established a kitchen in Chorbagan to feed the poor. Rajendra continued and improved his father's philanthropic interests, and the family also continues this tradition, feeding 300 people a day from their private trust fund.

According to the Mullick family, all the governors of India have been entertained in the ballroom of the Marble Palace, and India's top dancers have performed there. In 1858, a thousand and one candles glowed in the Venetian chandeliers of the ballroom as wigged and powdered men led ladies wearing crinolined gowns in a quadrille, while the gilt-framed mirrors of the great room reflected the glittering scene.

Rajah Rajendra Mullick's many achievements are embodied in the intriguing Marble Palace. Perhaps the most important is the inclusion of a binding clause in the trust deed which prevents any changes or additions to the original building. In this way, today's Mullick family can keep the palace alive by making it available as a museum, showcasing the family's vast collection of artefacts and allowing visitors a glimpse into the home of one of Calcutta's Great Families. In the words of Hirendro Mullick, custodian of the Marble Palace, the family is 'only an instrument'.

Ornamental stone seats, staues and fountains dot the gardens.

Tradition and Identity

Splendid Ruins, Architectural Expression and Independence

The Basu House or Basu Bari, as it is known, is one of Calcutta's most fascinating Great Houses. Located in the area of Bagbazar, which was once an exclusive district and the home of many wealthy aristocrats, it is an example of the city's lost heritage. Despite its neglected state, even today, palaces like Basu Bari are known as raj baris.

This enigmatic building is hard to find. Originally it covered an area of fourteen acres and extended up to the Maratha Ditch Lane. But year after year of division and subdivision, the property has been drastically reduced. At the address on Bagbazar Street, there is no sign of the palace, as small hutments, shops, a restaurant and a school have all grown up around the building. With these encroachments, the Basu Bari seems to have retreated from the main road and taken shelter in a narrow lane. It comes as a surprise to reach the end of the lane and suddenly discover a row of monumental columns rising above dense growth of bougainvillea.

ABOVE (LEFT AND RIGHT): *Various views of the splendour and decay inside the cavernous* thakur dalan.

PAGES 60-61: *The* thakur dalan, *a courtyard of Basu Bari.*

The entire exterior of the palace is highly decorative and unusual. Each massive column is topped with a circle of lion's heads in relief rather than the more common scrolls or floral motifs seen in other Great Houses of the same period. Each lion's head is connected by double rows of beads shaped in stucco.

Islamic-style archways on the ground floor open to a number of small waiting rooms and storerooms, all show severe signs of decay from the rising damp. From here the courtyard is reached, and once inside, the sheer size of the structure becomes evident. Originally, the house boasted of four courtyards, the most magnificent

Left: *Exterior detail of the Basu Bari shows a blending of architectural influences.*

Storeroom outside the main courtyard of the Basu Bari.

being the main courtyard with the *thakur dalan*. This is a dream-like space, beautifully proportioned and lined with tall columns. Like most other houses of its kind, the courtyard is a traditional and an important part of the house. Here various religious and family ceremonies were performed, such as the Jagaddhatri Puja, the first rice ceremony for a child and, of course, the Durga Puja.

Rooms run off from three sides of this rectangular space; to the east, west and south. However, it is the northern end, which draws the eye. Here the traditionally placed *thakur dalan* sits atop ascending steps, where six colossal fluted pillars introduce the worship platform and support the roof and parapet.

Behind this, intricate ornate Gothic style archways with Mughal and ancient Bengali influences form a line, through which the dark, cavernous interior is reached. It is most unusual in comparison to the more typical Hindu temple-like façades.

Although the walls are 700 millimetres thick, the area is poorly maintained and most of the structure is bare stonework, however, deep inside the worship area, traces of highly decorative murals and reliefs show the original turquoise and amber paintwork, and create a rich layered effect. Murals of Shiva, Durga, Maheswar, Brahma and Parvati can still be seen, as also some showing battle scenes from the Ramayana and Mahabharata. Strangely, a number of the figures are dressed as British soldiers. Painted stucco medallions, an English embellishment, feature a series of faces. Various other murals decorate the area, although some are almost destroyed. It has been many decades since the palace staged a Durga Puja ceremony.

Apart from an elegant sitting room on the ground floor, which is still grandly furnished and in good condition, there is very little that remains of the interior. Although the carpets have long since gone, the room is comfortable with large ornately carved armchairs, marble side-tables and statues and potted palms. Enormous oil paintings of the Basu's ancestors line the room in gilt frames, a number of them painted by artist Bamapada Mukherji. The house once boasted of a gold ceiling, large chandeliers and twenty-four-feet-high walls in the grand hall. A dancing room on the second floor included a stage, rows of chairs for guests and a *zenana* on the upper level from where the ladies and children of the house could watch the activity below.

Bengali engineer, Nilmoni Mitra was employed to design Basu's Great House. Mitra is thought to have built six or seven other grand homes in Bagbazar, however, his design for the Basu Bari is noteworthy. By mid-nineteenth century, the Great Houses of many affluent Bengalis had begun to feature European designs. However, rather than looking towards British architecture, with the Basu Bari Mitra seemed more inspired by traditional Bengali temples, mosques and sprawling rural estates. In the

design, Mitra managed to create a residential urban palace unlike any other.

The palace has an interesting and colourful history, beginning with the three Basu brothers: Mohendra, Nandalal and Pashupati. From humble beginnings, their fortunes changed suddenly in 1874, when their uncle passed away and Mohendra inherited a large part of Gaya, his enormous zamindari estate. After Mohendra's death, Nandalal and Pashupati began building the palace with their inheritance. According to the Basu family, the foundation stone was laid in October 1876 and the family began residing there two years later.

Pages 64-65: *Massive exterior columns of the Basu Bari.*

The Basu Bari appears at the end of a lane.

Despite enjoying an extravagant lifestyle typical of North Calcutta's wealthy Babus, Nandalal was also very religious, which led to many well-known spiritual figures visiting the palace, including the celebrated Ramakrishna. As Nandalal supervised the building, it is probable that his beliefs played a part in the quantity of religious motifs scattered throughout the palace, such as the hand-painted Kalighat-style images of Hindu gods and goddesses that decorate the French doors in the main sitting room.

Pashupati, though religious, loved theatre and the arts. Subsequently, these cultural pursuits led to famous actors and playwrights visiting the grand home, including Girish Ghosh. It is said that the *Victory of Pandavas* was performed here for Wazid Ali

Approach to the hidden Basu Bari.

Shah, the last ruler of Awadh, who was held captive by the British in Metiabruz, Calcutta. Religion and theatre, wealth and position, extravagance and pleasure, are all embodied in Basu's Great House.

The nineteenth century was a significant period for upper-class Indians like the Basu brothers. These merchant princes enjoyed Calcutta's Babu culture, and during the first half of the century much of their lifestyle could be identified as European. However, as the century wore on, particularly in the last quarter, many changes occurred and there was a reaction against the British. From then on, many Great Families, including the Basus, became more involved in the growing tide for freedom and the push for independence from Britain. Patriotism became a new and important part of Basu Bari's history.

It could be said that this change is embodied in the architecture of Basu Bari, which lacks significant

Sonali Basu and her daughter in the ancestral sitting room.

European architectural details typical of similar residences. Whether instructed by the Basus to remain true to more indigenous traditional designs thus illustrating anti-British sentiments, or whether Nilmoni Mitra was dictated simply by his own taste and style, we cannot be sure. However, the patronage of the Basu brothers did allow Mitra to demonstrate his creativity, producing a unique structure, without the need to copy the style and taste of the British.

With their growing political concerns, the Great House entertained many famous political leaders, including Surendra Nath Banerji, who gave lectures in front of the *thakur dalan* and held a meeting on the lawn during the Bengal Partition Movement. In fact, part of the freedom movement began in the palace. Amit Basu remembers the grand political functions, anti-British meetings and rallies and describes his grandfather as a freedom fighter whose political sentiments meant he was never considered for the title of rajah, a title Amit feels he would have declined.

Amit remembers his ancestral home coming alive with other grand functions, festivals and ceremonies: 'In the old days, when I was a boy, there were fifteen to twenty adult family members living here. We were all fed from a joint kitchen, we all lunched together. Sometimes my grandmother would sit with twenty or more grandchildren in a circle around her and feed each one by hand. I remember lots of Durga Puja ceremonies in the house and many servants. There was even a servant employed just to maintain the clocks!' These days Amit, his wife Sonali and their two children live in a comfortable new house built some thirty-five years ago by Amit's father. Interestingly, this large house,

on three levels, has been built inside one of the palace courtyards!

From the outside, the magnificent ruined façade of the Basu Bari is a sad reminder of its former opulent life and past glories. It is difficult to imagine there was once a large garden with fountains, a stable and even a zoo. Despite obvious pride in their heritage home, the Basus find it difficult to maintain, let alone restore. Family disputes and the difficulty in maintaining such a large home has forced the family to gift part of the house and many artefacts to the Kolkata Municipal Corporation. It is hoped that with the help of the government, these heritage treasures will be restored and maintained, something that now seems impossible to achieve in private hands.

Arched doorways from the entrance to the outer rooms.

European Style in Calcutta

The Maharajah of Burdwan's City Palace

By the late nineteenth century, many wealthy merchants and landowners had totally embraced the architecture and style of Europe. The Burdwan Palace on Diamond Harbour Road, South Calcutta, is a fine example of the ways in which Calcutta's aristocracy was influenced by their colonial rulers. More a grand European mansion than a palace, it was designed for lavish entertaining in the English manner, rather than traditional religious family gatherings. European influences removed inner courtyards and replaced them with ballrooms and Victorian tables and chairs.

Once the palace boasted of large grounds and gardens, which extended to the street, but today, a simple driveway leads the way through the many buildings that have sprung up on the land which the family was forced to sell after Independence. Calico-draped hoardings attempt to disguise the untidy approach until the dramatic deep yellow mansion comes into view with its long, elegant entrance porch supported by fluted

Ball room of the Burdwan Palace, now only the chandeliers remain.

Below: *Shuttered doors open on to the verandahs.*

Pages 70-71: *The magnificient Burdwan Palace on Diamond Harbour Road.*

Corinthian columns. The Burdwan coat of arms sits proudly on an impressive pedimental façade.

The Burdwan Raj was founded by Abu Raj Kapur of Lahore in 1657 and his descendents have served under both the Mughal emperors and the British government. At one time, the Maharajah of Burdwan was the premier nobleman of lower Bengal, with over 3,00,000 tenant-farmers in an area of some 8,000 square miles. They owe their former great wealth to Maharajah Chand Mahtab, who was adept in managing the family's vast land holdings or zamindaris. His loyalty to the British during the Santhal rebellion of 1855 and the Uprising of 1857 was rewarded with the grant of a coat of arms and the right to a personal salute of thirteen guns.

His adopted son, Maharajah Bijay Chand Mahtab, who succeeded his father in 1888, also gained distinction with the British by risking his life to save Sir Andrew Fraser, the lieutenant governor of Bengal, during an assassination attempt in 1908.

The Burdwan family lost much of their land in East Bengal due to the Partition. The majority of the Burdwan estates, consisting of up to ten of the country palaces, tea gardens and mines became part of Bangladesh. The family never got over the loss. With no income the family estates could not survive, despite the new nation state inviting them to remain. Offers of purchase from the government were so low that the Maharajah decided to donate the country palaces and gardens to the government to be used for a university. Today, the former Maharajah's palace in the rural district of Burdwan, sixty-seven miles north-west of Calcutta, is the main educational institution of the area and is still supported by the Maharajah's estate.

Entrance to the palace.

ABOVE: *An elegant balcony in the Burdwan Palace.*

As the marble plaque 'Bijay Manzil' attests in Persian on the entrance gate, it was Maharajah Bijay Chand Mahtab who built the Diamond Harbour Road mansion. Today, most of the rooms are empty.

At present, the Maharajah's granddaughter, Princess Karuna Devi, is the only descendent living in the palace. Her apartments face the garden and a large tank, around which the stables once stood. Today, it is surrounded by high-rise apartment buildings. Her elegantly furnished rooms are hung with oil paintings, including an image of her grandfather, and antique tables display framed photographs of other ancestors. The partly enclosed verandah is furnished with comfortable chairs and potted palms. It is a restful place to sit and sip tea from a tray brought by her personal maid. Karuna remembers the palace in its hey days with visiting viceroys and other dignitaries; the beautifully kept coaches and horses; the family elephants being kept outside Calcutta only; travelling between their

Cast iron balustrades of the double staircase, the entry hall.

Below: *Ornate ceiling of the dining room, known as the 'Chinese Room'.*

Page 74:
Left: *Princess Karuna Devi of the Burdwan Raj (seated), with her sister.*

Pages 74-75:
Right: *Comfortable, European-style verandah in the Burdwan Palace.*

country palace and the city villa, and during the heat of summer, staying in their grand home in Darjeeling and riding to school every day; and the exciting new tradition of cocktail parties beginning in Calcutta after World War II.

The beautiful semi-circular balcony, the setting for many photo shoots, is the same as is the tiny verandah room used for the movie *City of Joy*. However, the rest of the mansion is now empty and silent. The magnificent stairway leads to empty rooms after empty rooms, all of elegant proportions. Fan-lights, French doors and ornate Belgian chandeliers in deep reds and greens are the only features left of these buildings once so full of life. The famous 'Chinese Room' is now used to store dusty, broken furniture, and the tiger skins and marble tables that once graced the ballroom are long gone.

The Burdwan coat of arms.

Thanthania, the Great House of the Laha Family

In North Calcutta, the Laha family lives in four of Calcutta's Great Houses, on over seven acres of land. In earlier times, wealthy families would buy nearby land or properties for family members. Despite the Bengali tradition of living in joint families, even large mansions and palaces eventually became too small for growing families.

Thanthania, a relatively 'new' house and named after the sound produced by Indian temple bells, is 175 years old, painted deep red and set close behind a high fence. It is home to younger family members, including Aloke Laha, his wife and children. The older house, some 300 years old and built before the arrival of the British, is occupied by the older members of the family and connected to Thanthania by a complicated series of alleys and staircases, once used by the large retinue of servants needed to maintain a Great House.

A small cantilever verandah breaks the façade of the building, which features arched windows and Calcutta's ubiquitous green shutters. It could seem austere in

RIGHT: *Aloke Laha in the grand courtyard at Thanthania.*

BELOW: *The old and new palace, side by side.*

PAGES 78-79: *Intricate black-and-white archways of the courtyard at Thanthania.*

Colourful exterior, the Laha family's Thanthania.

comparison with other Great Houses, however, on entering the building, visitors are immediately struck by the ornate black-and-cream wrought iron double staircase, which takes up the entire entrance area. Upstairs, hallways lead to a verandah, which offers a view of the magnificent main courtyard. This dramatic black-and-white space is heavily embellished with stucco ornamentation above multiple fluted archways and a marble floor in the *thakur dalan*.

Small arched windows on the second level, the *zenana*, feature delicate fretwork and balance the heavier lower archways. This is the first of the three grand courtyards, and it is here that Aloke Laha remembers playing cricket as a young boy.

The *thakur dalan* is the most important part of a Great House and Thanthania is no exception. Every

ABOVE (TOP AND BOTTOM): *Goddess Kali and other deities in the puja room.*

RIGHT: *Ornate display of worship in a Great House.*

second year the Lahas host a traditional Durga Puja ceremony when the family deity, made of gold and knick-named 'Jayjayman', is in residence. Thanthania has special rooms for the deity, who moves to other family members' homes each year.

Durga Puja is Calcutta's most important religious festival. Astrologers are consulted even on the auspicious time for performing puja. The Laha family invites their relatives and guests to the festival, where the goddess is worshipped for four days. Special food and offerings are prepared and guests offer sweets to the deity.

Aloke enjoys the closeness of his family members but understands it is difficult to maintain in a modern world: 'Joint families are less these days... people want more privacy and also cannot afford big houses with the servants needed to run them. In the old days, all the garden gates would stay open and people came and went freely. Now the garden gates are kept shut. Life has changed; sixty years ago it was a traditional way of living and dressing. There were no turbans in Calcutta... that is the dress of the Punjabis... in Calcutta it was a dhoti and kurta. We kept a horse and carriage, and many servants. It was a grand way of life.'

On the roof of Thanthania the extent of the other houses can be seen, including the garden and walls that divide the properties,

Walkways connecting the houses.

where so many aunts, uncles and cousins live that Aloke cannot be sure of the exact number.

Milon Datta and his family live in one of these houses. Thanthania Datta Bari on Bidhan Sarani is an enormous rambling house built on many levels, with two main courtyards and a number of smaller open spaces divided by narrow dark corridors and flights of stairs, some leading to just a few rooms. It is the kind of house children would love to explore.

The Datta family is a branch of the Laha family, who became wealthy by trading in cotton, spice and jute bales. They then increased their wealth even further by owning jute mills, tea gardens and zamindaris. The extent of their properties included a grand house in Barrackpore on the Ganges with beautiful marble stairs leading to the riverbank. They also owned large areas of Midnapore and more land towards the Sunderbans. However, after Independence the new Indian Government took almost all of their vast land holdings. Like many Great Families, the Dattas tried to fight back, but due to the legal costs of litigation, lost 160 of the family's houses.

Milon is the fifth generation of Dattas, but an amazing six generations live in the house today. The founder of this Great Family, Dwarka Nath Dutt, was just twenty-six when he built the house in 1850, and the first Durga Puja was celebrated in 1855. The continuation of the Durga Puja ceremony is very important and their family trust fund is in the name of their deities. In fact, the family sees themselves as caretakers of their Great House and feel that 'God is the real owner'. The Durga Puja ceremony has always been a vital element of the Great Houses' traditions, not only for the religious aspects, but also as a means to show off their wealth and position. In earlier times, the ceremony was seen as a barometer of their status.

Since India's Independence, Calcutta's remaining residential mansions and palaces seem caught in a relentless process of decay. However, a few of these magnificent buildings like Thanthania, survive and are maintained in almost original form. They reflect the opulence, grandeur and power of Calcutta's former aristocrats. Apart from a few modernising elements, the buildings, the neighbourhood and the domestic lifestyle of the inhabitants remain to a considerable extent, unchanged. As more and more of Calcutta's splendid palaces and mansions decline, the Laha and Datta families' Great Houses offer valuable insights into a way of life that is becoming increasingly lost.

PAGE 84:
TOP: *Rooftops of multiple family mansions.*

MIDDLE: *Milon Datta with his aunt on the steps of the* thakur dalan *of Datta Bari.*

BOTTOM: Thakur dalan.

Washing day on a walkway of the Laha mansion.

১৩৩৫
শ্রীশ্রী ৺ বিন্ধ্যবাসিনী
মাতা
1928

The Power of the Image

The Deity at Home, Religion and Everyday Life

The most important festival for the city of Calcutta is the Durga Puja. For days the city comes alive with light, colour and sound to worship the ten-armed goddess who represents divine power over all evil. It is not only a religious festival, but also a time for generosity and hospitality during social and family gatherings and the whole city gets caught up in the magic and gaiety.

Months before the Durga Puja commences, the city's artists begin their work in the small lanes of Kumartuli, North Calcutta. Generations of skilled artisans with the surname 'Pals', have been creating clay goddesses here for centuries, and their work is highly respected. The process begins simply, with bamboo sticks of various shapes and sizes tied together and shaped with jute strings to form the basic structure. The next stage is the application of clay, which is supplied by labourers who swim underwater to gather it from the riverbed. The clay is then applied in three stages, the last process involving pieces of cloth soaked in water from the Ganges being applied to the joints of the goddess

to prevent it from cracking after the drying process. When complete the goddess is painted and the final touches, such as lips and eyes are given by the most experienced artists. The entire figure is then varnished, a jute wig glued on, dressed and decorated and made ready for worship in the many displays or pandals, that are constructed on every street corner of the city. The whole city supports these displays, where people of all ages gather to worship, listen to the musicians or simply take in the beauty of their goddess.

The culmination of the community Durga Puja is the immersion of the goddess in the holy waters of the Ganges. In this way, the clay deities return to the river where they began and the Kumartuli artisans begin their painstaking work all over again.

Two hundered and fifty years ago, the Great Houses gained prominence for the religious devotion and extravagance of their traditional household as well as community Durga Puja ceremonies. Today, the continuation of the Durga Puja is still important and imparts a great sense of pride to all the Great Families who manage to remain in their ancestral homes.

Religion is also important on a daily basis and the Great Houses are the site of traditional daily devotion, and age-old religious traditions. Unlike the community ceremonies, the Great Families do not immerse their deity but rather retain them lovingly for centuries. When there are a number of houses in the family, the deity will spend an equal amount of time with each.

Pradeep and Servina Guptoo's family home is an example of the care and attention given to the family deity. One of Calcutta's Great Families, the Guptoos' home takes up an entire city block in one of Calcutta's

Left: *Special marble altar of the Guptoos' family deity when 'in residence'.*

Below: *Garlanding the deity with fresh flowers is another daily ritual.*

Page 88:
Top: *Betel leaf-shaped clay candle holders for worship.*

Middle and Bottom: *Potters of Kurmartuli busy preparing the clay deities.*

Pages 86-87: *Ornate and colourful temple courtyard in North Calcutta.*

busiest commercial areas, Middleton Road. Like many old homes in Calcutta, high taxes have resulted in the selling off of land, either as a whole or piece by piece to save the house itself.

The Guptoos' home is now virtually swallowed up by the city, completely hidden from view by shop-fronts and commercial buildings. From the street there is no indication that the house exists at all and visitors must find their crowded driveway and squeeze past a collection of vintage cars before entering the house.

The rambling home is a comfortable mix of antique English and Indian furniture set against classic Roman columns and Calcutta's green shutters. Eight adults and six children live in this warm family home, which was originally built for Bishop Middleton at the end of the nineteenth century.

TOP RIGHT: *A room for the Guptoos' family deity.*

Unique upper-level courtyard for women in Guptoos' home.

The family's ancestral home in North Calcutta is still occupied by Pradeep's cousins. Pradeep's great grandfather decided to move his family to the city's European area after being ostracised from his community for his work as a surgeon. When Bishop Middleton moved to St. Paul's in Chowringhee, the house in Middleton Road became available and the family moved to Calcutta's White Town. As Pradeep's great grandfather was the first Indian to do such a thing, it caused a sensation and people protested to the government and the scandal was published in the newspapers of the day.

The mansion has an unusual light and bright courtyard on the second level, the area normally used for the *zenana*, which was usually kept dark. Traditionally, the womenfolk spent their days on the first floor, out of sight, whiling away the hours hidden behind their screened verandahs, watching the activity in the courtyard below. According to family history, Pradeep's grandmother was a strong-minded woman and insisted on having a courtyard for the women of the family. Her considerate husband agreed to her wishes and built a courtyard for her.

Today, Pradeep and Servina's children play cricket in the upstairs courtyard, 'smashing windowpanes and masonry regularly!' Pradeep adds, 'the house is in a constant state of repair! Servants come and go. I don't know if they live in or not!' The roof of the home is its religious heart and an integral part of the Guptoos' daily life. A series of large, cool rooms sit on the rooftop and house the apartments of the family deity. Black and white marble floors and beautiful polished timber cupboards house a collection of copper and brass cooking pots and platters, paralleling the family kitchen below. Each year the deity moves between the various Guptoo family members who take turns in treating her as part of the family.

A courtyard in the mansion of the Datta family.

RIGHT: *Four-poster bed fit for a deity.*

RIGHT: *The family temple on the grounds of the Biswas mansion, Cossipore.*

An everyday altar.

Left: *Beautiful hall leading to the deity's room - Roys of Behala.*

Below: *The* tulsi mancha, *considered auspicious, stands at the entrance to the deity's room.*

The family have been worshipping the deity ever since Pradeep's ancestor found it and brought it to Calcutta from his village, generations ago. When in residence at Middleton Road, a special marble altar is used for the hand-sized deity, and each night she is placed comfortably in a miniature four-poster bed complete with bed linen, velvet quilt and mosquito netting. In addition, the Guptoos hold a daily puja at sunset to worship Lakshmi, the Goddess of Well-Being.

During colonial times, the Great Houses were the setting for expensive, large-scale Durga Puja festivals. As the fortunes of Calcutta's great merchant families began to decline, so did the practice, and the communities began to hold their own. This practice grows more elaborate and competitive every year. However, a number of Great Families do manage to continue the tradition of holding Calcutta's most important religious festival in their ancestral homes.

Ruined and Forgotten, the Andul Raj Bati

To reach the Andul Raj Bati, the frenetic city of Calcutta is left behind. Situated in Howrah, a quieter district on the eastern side of River Hooghly, Andul is reached by crossing the Howrah Bridge, now Rabindra Setu. This 1,500-feet-long cantilever bridge carries approximately two million people a day and a wide assortment of vehicles. Once across, there is a decided change of pace. Tiny huts, roadside stalls and palm trees line the thirty-kilometre-road to Andul, a sleepy, relaxed village where street vendors display fresh fruits and vegetables on banana leaves. In this tropical landscape, far from the pollution and traffic of Calcutta, the magnificent but forgotten Andul Palace sits a little removed from the main street, behind high walls and a triumphant arched gateway.

At first sight, the sheer size of the Andul Palace is overwhelming. A row of ten massive Doric columns forms the façade, each with a radius of twenty feet. Although in a sad state of decay, the 100-room palace is magnificent in the mellow bronze of the afternoon light, its flaws hidden for a moment in time.

Unlike the crowded lanes of North Calcutta, the Andul Palace is set on extensive green lawns. On closer inspection, these lawns are marked out as playing fields for the sporting club of a local school, the Satadal Institution, which rents a large number of the palace rooms. Other rooms are rented out to a variety of tenants. On the steps, washing is laid out to dry and a lady sits in the sun brushing her long hair.

This historic family dates back to the founder, Ramcharan Roy (1720-70), who worked as a dewan for the British East India Company in the 1740s and attracted the attention of Robert Clive. With a Persian and Arabic education, as well as some knowledge of English, Ramcharan rose in Clive's esteem and like Raja Nabakrishna Deb, enjoyed the patronage of the British rulers. The Battle of Plassey and the subsequent rise in power of the British improved the position and prospects of almost every senior employee of the East India Company, including Ramcharan Roy.

When Shah Alam, the Mughal emperor, bestowed titles, Lord Clive recommended Ramcharan Roy. However, he

Ruined exterior of the Andul Raj Bati.

RIGHT: *Shuttered doors open on to a derelict verandah.*

PAGES 94-95: *A view of the magnificent exterior of the Andul Raj Bati.*

refused the honour for himself, instead asking that his eldest son Ramlochon Roy be given the title as he felt he was more worthy of the distinction. Subsequently, the title of 'rajah' was bestowed on his son in January 1766 and Rajah Ramlochon Roy was given command of 4,000 troops.

The young rajah improved his family's palace, installing a marble overlaid dance floor, Belgian chandeliers, a Durga *dalan*, silver wall pieces and numerous oil paintings. The family maintains that Raja Ramlochon was among the first Bengalis of a Great House to send an invitation, carved in ivory, to Lord Clive, inviting him to attend the palace's first grand Durga Puja held in 1770. Clive accepted, arriving on horseback with thirty of his friends. He is noted as having enjoyed the evening in 'perfect paradise'.

Preparation for the Durga Puja festival was an elaborate affair at the Andul Palace. Painters and Patuas from Krishnanagar worked for six weeks, creating and wrapping the goddess, an *ekchala pratima* in silver foil. The *Ashtami bhog* comprised some eighty different kinds of sweet-meats, 200 different varieties of fruits and *motichoor ladoo*s in the shape of canon balls. Around 20,000 people ate in the palace for five consecutive days and at the time of the *Shandhi* Puja over 100 silver lamps were lit and several cannons were fired. On Shaptami morning, a Scottish highland band

Above: *Ruined columns of the palace ballroom.*

Below: The palace canon.

from Fort William accompanied the *kalabou* for her ritualistic bath in the Saraswati River. There was a saying in those days, that the goddess would come to visit and eat from the hands of Rajah Ramlochon, as he offered her a feast fit for a queen.

Today, Rajah Pradeep Kumar Mitra, advocate of the High Court of Calcutta and the great grandson of Raja Khestra Krishna Mitra, his wife, daughter and uncle, live in a series of comfortable, though not grand, rooms in an isolated part of the palace. Like many former aristocrats, the Mitras find themselves in a strange and difficult situation.Whether titled from birth or having titles bestowed on them by the British makes no difference, as families who carry the names of their influential ancestors, must adapt to a world which cares little for former aristocrats, let alone their crumbling, faded palaces and mansions.

A once magnificent, but now derelict staircase of Burma teak leads to the Mitras' apartments. Even though the palace is in decline, afternoon tea is served in a buttercup yellow living room filled with comfortable floral sofas and paintings of ancestors on the walls. Pradeep explains the difficulty of living in a 'Great House' as

descendants of an ancient royal family: 'Life has changed for us considerably. We are proud of our history but it is impossible to maintain a building of this size without support. Our lifestyle and traditions have been curtailed and the only tradition we continue is the Durga Puja, now in its 234th year, and the everyday Annapurna Puja, which costs 10,000 rupees a month. The money comes from what is left of the Andul State property, so the traditional Durga Puja has had to be cut down considerably.'

The sheer size of the palace makes it obviously impossible to be maintained in private hands. In 1990, the building was declared a heritage site by the West Bengal government's heritage department. However, the department has not had the funds for restoration or maintenance. Despite the family's pride in their ancestry and ancestral home, Pradeep finds it ironic that the palace has a heritage title when the building is falling to pieces.

'Most of the rooms are locked up now, even though they have been used in films such as Satyajit Ray's *Jalshaghar* and *Sahib Bibi Ghulam*. Sadly, the magnificent

FACING PAGE:
ABOVE: *Temple of the Andul Raj Bati.*

BELOW: *Entrance to the Temple.*

ABOVE: *Wooden letter boxes of the Mitras.*

PAGES 98-99: *Buttercup yellow living room, Andul Raj Bati.*

PREVIOUS PAGE 99: *Former rajah, Pradeep Kumar Mitra.*

RIGHT: *Large and simply furnished bedroom in the Andul Raj Bati.*

BELOW: *A functional sitting room.*

dance floor is now completely ruined and most of the time there is no electricity.'

The situation is difficult and a common problem for the present generation of the Great Families. Pradeep has repeatedly asked the government to turn the palace into a medical college or a university; however, his proposals have fallen on deaf ears. 'The moment they agree we will be only too glad to leave, although we don't know where we will go.' There is also constant pressure from promoters to sell off the land that surrounds the palace, however, the Mitras know that once the land goes, so will the palace. Pride and honour keeps them hanging on although the situation seems hopeless.

Compared to Calcutta's city palaces, this aristocratic rural family is respected in the surrounding villages, having never abandoned their land or their people. When Pradeep walks through the town, well-wishers

appear constantly. 'I'm still referred to as *Rajbarirchele*, successor of the rajah's house, by the people in the area. They look up to me. I am made chief guest at weddings and functions, and I am asked to be president of local clubs and charitable institutions... it means a lot to me, but that is where the glamour ends.'

View of Andul from the rooftop of the palace.

Country Life in Rural Bengal

The Great Families who were landowners or zamindars divided their time between their city mansions and their sprawling country estates. Some rural properties were so vast and wealthy that they were ruled independently, like the princes or maharajahs of the ruling class, who had their own courts, tax collectors and police force. The early palaces and ways of life within owed much to Mughal culture, with separate areas, such as the *zenana*, within the confines of the estate itself.

The Palace of Maheshadal

The palace of Maheshadal is a fine example of the spaciousness of these rural estates and the number of buildings within its boundaries. Descendents of this zamindari family believe their palace is the 'only real palace in Bengal'. It is certainly an impressive sight, standing alone surrounded by a lush, semi-tropical garden rather than the dense urban sprawl of North Calcutta. The family's ancestor Anandadulal Upadhaya

came from Uttar Pradesh and took the name Maheshadal from the name of his village.

The palace shows classical and colonial features, as well as the influence of central Indian architecture in its hybrid design. Multiple wide hallways feature throughout, unlike the small, dark passageways of North Calcutta's mansions. There is also an absence of shutters; instead fine fretwork is set into many of the window frames. The outer rooms are light and airy and open on to a semi-circular verandah decorated with a beautiful marble-topped table and scattered bench seats. It would be very pleasant to while the days away

Above: *The verandah of the Maheshadal Palace.*

Pages 104-105: *The Maheshadal Palace.*

The trophy room inside the Maheshadal Palace.

Below: *The original palace of Maheshadal, c. 1857.*

in quiet contemplation in this airy space, miles from the busy city of Calcutta.

Inside, the palace is decorated more formally, the grand reception room resplendent with velvet curtains, throne-like chairs and ancestral paintings. Delving further into the palace the trophy room is reached, where stuffed tigers, bears and antelopes line the walls. The walls of a Great House often displayed trophies such as these as big game hunting was a sport of the rajahs and nawabs, the landed gentry, for centuries.

Surprisingly, the huge palace was built as a guest house in 1900, overtaking the original palace of 1857 in style, size and grandeur. As a guest house, the palace does not include a *zenana*, nor does it include a courtyard. However, not all zamindari houses had courtyards as these large estates had their own temples

The Radhagobindo Temple at Maheshadal.

nearby, where the deity could be worshipped by the family as well as the villagers.

It was the move to densely populated North Calcutta which developed the need for privacy and fresh air in the form of the courtyard. The deity of the Maheshadal family resides in the beautiful Radhagobindo Temple nearby.

There are a number of other mansions on the estate, including an ornate pavilion-style building for the Brahmin priests who looked after the religious requirements of the family and the temple. Numerous guards were employed to man the fortifications that were built around the estate.

Today, most of the buildings on the estate are under lock and key. Eighty-six-year-old Maharani Kaliyar Dala Devi is the only member of the family living in the palace.

When describing the house of a zamindar, Lal Behai Day wrote in 1920:

> always the largest and the finest in a village, facing south to avoid the north wind in winter and catch the pleasant south wind in summer...

and further;

> The hall was covered with carpets, where the zamindar would sit, propped up on pillows while officials would squat at varying distances according to their rank...
>
> ...the *dalan* was only used on great religious festivals when deity images were placed there, and dramatics and pantomimes were made in the open

One of the many mansions on the estate grounds at Maheshadal.

Above: *A house for priests where religious items were kept.*

courtyard below, which was covered with a large cloth canopy, called a 'moonshade'...

...beyond the *dalan-badi* a third courtyard of exactly the same area featured a covered verandah on all sides, similar to the design of the *dalan-badi*; two stories high, containing a large number of small rooms, with very few windows. This part of the house was the women's apartments, called the inner chamber, *andar-mahal* or the *zenana*, an area exclusively for the women of the house.'

The heady lifestyles of the zamindars have long gone. In the case of the Maheshadal palace and estate, we can only see the faded remnants, the remains of a way of life long gone and almost forgotten.

The later entrance gate, built in the early to mid-nineteenth century.

Top: *The ancient entrance gate to the Garhbari, Bansberia.*

Right (above): *A view of the palace moat.*

Right (Bottom): *The Garhbari Palace with wall and embankment.*

The Hangseshwari Temple, with the Vasudeva Temple on the left.

The Garhbari

The palace of this rural estate is called the Garhbari or moat house which describes the deep moat and high embankments that surround the property. Built in the early nineteenth century, the palace is also surrounded by a high wall and guardhouses at the front and rear, fitted with watchtowers and canon, necessary to deter invaders in earlier times.

Kanak Roy tells of his ancestor, Rajah Rameswar, who built the terracotta Temple of Vesudeva, which can be seen clearly from the terrace of the palace. Even though it was built in 1679, it still stands today and is famous for its murals.

The beautiful Hangseshwari Temple, also well known, was built in 1815 in the *ratha ratna* or pinnacled style. With six stories and thirteen turrets in the shape of lotus buds, it is a remarkable sight. It is in this temple that the family's deity resides.

Today, the palace is home to Kanak Roy and his brother, the descendents of Rajah Rameswar. The brothers live in leisured isolation with just a few servants in attendance.

The Burdwan Estate, Burdwan

The Burdwan Raj can be dated from the reign of Aurangzeb (1658–1707). The Burdwan titles and privileges were bestowed by the Mughul emperors.

The Palace of the Maharajah of Burdwan.

FACING PAGE:
ABOVE: *A mansion on the former Burdwan estate.*

BELOW: *The* Golapbag, *or 'garden of roses', the former Burdwan estate.*

The Maharajah of Burdwan occupied a position similar to a feudal prince right up to the early days of British rule in India, when he was still treated as a semi-independent native ruler, with a prestigious social and political position, which included civil and military administration powers. The Burdwan Raj occupied a landed area of over 10,310 square kilometres and was founded by Abu Rai who settled in the district of Burdwan around 1657.

In its hey day, the Burdwan Raj owned properties which included Mahtab Manzil, the palace in Burdwan; Bijay Manzil, the palace in Kolkata, shown in another chapter of this book; Dilram and the Dar-ul-Bahan, mansions in Burdwan; the Rajbati in Kalna; The Rosebank in Darjeeling; The Retreat in Kurseong; and many other residences in Varanasi, Kanpur, Cuttack and more.

Entrance to the Somra Palace.

In Burdwan town, in the district of Burdwan, the maharajahs Chand Mahtab and Bijay Chand Mahtab contributed to making the area culturally and economically stronger, which included the setting up and the support of the Burdwan Raj College. When the estate was brought under the Permanent Settlement, the revenue paid to the imperial treasury by the Burdwan estates was one of the largest in India.

Today, the Rajbati or palace of the maharajah, is utilised for the administration of the university while academic activities centre on the mansions and gardens of the maharajah known as the *Golapbag* or rose garden.

Left: *The large courtyard of the Somra Palace.*

Below: *The Somra Palace beside the lake.*

The Somra Palace, Somra

The Somra Palace is in a severe state of disrepair. An elderly couple lives in the dilapidated building, acting as caretakers, but the family have moved on, coming to their ancestral home just a few times a year, in particular during the time of the Durga Puja. Set in a beautiful location beside a lake, the palace looks across to an ancient and exquisite terracotta temple. In the afternoon sun the whole area has a magical glow, with a family of ducks the only disturbance.

The entrance to the double-storied palace is partly overtaken by vegetation but six Doric columns forming a shallow portico can be seen. The columns and façade of the palace are simple, timber rafters over the entrance show there was once a roof, long since gone. The entrance is dark and tunnel-like, similar in style to the entrances to many North Calcutta palaces. Various storage rooms and offices run off the entrance before reaching an inner, grassy courtyard dominated by a raised *thakur dalan*

The Somra Kali Temple.

featuring five archways. The lower and upper levels again feature Doric columns of equal size, indicating the house was built as a whole, an indication of wealth. The upper-level-columns are separated by wrought iron railings and fixed wooden shutters above.

The courtyard is unusual as it has a smaller, delineated space within, created by short pillars, possibly the Doric columns cut to size, and linked by decorative wrought iron panels creating a smaller, square compound, with openings on the north and south sides. The pillars are topped by curved metal hooks overhanging the inner space. These were possibly used to hang containers of flowers or cloth shading. Overall, the decoration of the building is unadorned, and in this way differs from the sometimes over-decorated style of some of North Calcutta's palaces. There is little history to be found on this palace, however, it is helpful in understanding the decline of many wealthy zamindari estates in West Bengal. In this case, the pictures tell the story.

The rural palaces of Bengal are linked in many ways to their city counterparts. Many Great Families began as landowners or zamindars or were indirectly associated with zamindari backgrounds. Early rural and city palaces followed the Mughal style which includes the *zenana*, the sprawling estates, and their way of life and culture.

One of the major differences is that in Calcutta, size of land was often restricted, therefore, the palaces of the city's wealthy merchants and *bania*s incorporated worship areas, the *thakur dalan,* within the confines of the house itself, while the aristocratic rural families usually kept their deity in temples built separate to their palaces. By looking at the rural estates, we have a broader view of the life and times of the Great Families in the city and the country.

Intricate carvings on the walls of the Somra Temple.

End Note

...The late eighteenth and early nineteenth centuries were the setting for the first sustained encounter between Asian intellectuals and the West. An Indian intelligentsia living in Calcutta responded in a most creative way to aspects of European culture that became available to them.

P.J. Marshall, 2000.

An interesting location is often one that retains its originality, offering ways of seeing the past. Globalisation has robbed many cities of their individual characters, resulting in a blending of cultures and a loss of individuality. Calcutta, however, the most European-looking city in India, and also the least Western, is one of the few cities in the world that has retained its own unique and authentic character.

The area of North Calcutta exists much as it did in colonial times. A study of early maps shows that the original street patterns largely survived until the end of the nineteenth century. It is aspects like these

Above and Pages 118-19: Courtyards and arched colonnades were common features of the Great Houses.

which make it a fascinating area in which to explore the city's history and the heritage buildings of its extravagant merchants.

With no government body to oversee the designs, the sprawling, multiple courtyards, monumental ensembles, classical columns and European furnishings of the Great Houses show not only the architectural response to British buildings during colonial times, but also a large amount of individuality and exuberance.

Additional, unexpected features, such as the personal eccentricities or hobbies of the founders are embedded in the designs, translating into an eclectic whole that somehow manages to surprise and enchant.

In the nineteenth century, Calcutta developed to become the most important centre in India for modern education, science, culture and politics. It was the home of intellectuals, scientists and artists. However, during the decades after Independence, Calcutta lost its social and economic importance, and today, like other large cities, struggles with poverty, pollution and traffic congestion.

In comparison to other Indian cities, Calcutta is of fairly recent origin. In 1990 it celebrated its tercentenary. Within a little over three hundred years it has grown into one of the biggest cities in the world, with a teeming population and constant demand for additional space. Urban land holdings are being divided and sub divided constantly, and new built-up areas are being added to every day.

Despite this, there is no doubt that Calcutta will survive. It is a city that has managed through extreme circumstances, time after time, yet still retains its own eclectic charm and individuality. It would seem that Calcutta is and perhaps always will be an eccentric city of extremes.

Calcutta's past misfortunes certainly impacted on the Great Houses. Today, complicated trust funds, family disputes, tropical climate, threat of developers and lack of funds have taken their toll. The question remains: what is Calcutta to do with its Great Houses and can they survive in the twenty-first century despite their complex problems?

For an answer it would seem we must put our trust in this resourceful city. With its remarkable revolutionary history and new, increasing economic success, Calcutta simply needs the will to find a way to preserve this precious part of India's history and heritage.

Glossary

Ashtami bhog	food offered to the deity on *Ashtami* or eighth day of Durga Navaratri or third day of Durga Puja
Babu	man of distinction during the eighteenth century but as the nineteenth century wore on it became a derogatory term in Bengal to patronise the indigenous elites
bagh	garden or meadow
baithakhana	hall
bania	type of agent
bhadralok	'gentleman' class, from respectable middle class to wealthy elites
bustee	slum settlements, shantytowns
classical	Greco-Roman architecture
dacoit	dangerous robbers and criminals
dewan	principal administrator
Durga Puja	festival to worship Goddess Durga
ekchala pratima	deity of Durga and her family in a single frame
kalabou	banana tree draped in sari, considered very auspicious
kayastha	caste or class of scribes; their occupation, writers or accountants
lakh	one hundred thousand by Indian system of counting
mahal	palace
maidan	field; square; parade ground
mandap	hall; pillared pavilion; also refers to a temporary cloth structure
mandir	temple
mistri	master craftsman; carpenter
motichoor ladoo	typical Indian sweet made from gramflour
munshi	writer; secretary
nachghar	room for dancing
natmandir	hall opposite to *thakur dalan* meant for religious ceremonies
navaratna	ancient architecture featuring nine 'jewels' or brick pinnacles
nawab	nobleman; ruler; governor; generally, a Muslim term
Neo-classical	revivalist Greco-Roman architecture
palanquin	hand-held chair for carrying dignitaries

pandal	spectacular installation to house sculptures of deities during pujas
pediment	moulding of triangular form above an opening
plinth	block or slab base for a statue, column or wall
puja	worship; honour; veneration
puja room	prayer room or shrine
punkahs	ceiling fans made of cloth, suspended on a frame and operated manually
rajah/raj	rulers, the government
Raj Bari	literally 'ruler's house'; mansion with courtyard
sarkars	indigenous heads of European households
sati	widow throwing herself in her husband's funeral pyre, a practice prevalent in seventeenth-eighteenth-century Bengal
Shandhi puja	puja held when the *Ashtami* ends and the *Navami* begins
Shaptami	seventh day of the auspicious Durga Navaratri or second day of Durga Puja
subernabaniks	traditional merchant class of Calcutta
taluqdar	in Bengal, taluqdar is equal to zamindar in terms of land control and social status
tank	artificial water storage pond
thakur	Lord, title of respect
thakur dalan	area of worship or altar
zamindar	landlord; controls land, responsible for revenue payment to government
zenana	apartments for women in high-class Muslim and Hindu houses

Bibliography

Bhabha, H., *The Location of Culture*, London: Routeledge, 1994.

Busteed, H.E. *Echoes from Old Calcutta*, 1897.

Chattopadhyay, S. *Representing Calcutta, Modernity, Nationalism, and the Colonial Uncanny*, London: Routledge, 2005.

Cohn, B.S. *Colonialism and its Forms of Knowledge, the British in India*, New Jersey: Princeton University Press, 1996.

Chatterji, J. *Bengal Divided*, New Delhi: Cambridge University Press, 1995.

Chaudhuri, S. ed., *Calcutta: The Living City, Vol.1: The Past*, Delhi: Oxford University Press, 1990.

———. ed., *Calcutta: The Living City, Vol. 2: The Present and the Future*, Delhi: Oxford University Press, 1990.

Dasgupta, K. 'A City away from home: mapping of Calcutta', in *Texts of Power, Emerging Disciplines in Colonial Bengal*, Partha Chatterjee (ed.), Minnesota: University of Minnesota Press, 1995.

Day, Rev. L.B. *Bengal Peasant Life*, London: Macmillan and Co., 1920.

Deb, Raja B.K., *The Early History and Growth of Calcutta*, Calcutta: Anu Press, 1905.

Dutta, K. *Calcutta, a Cultural and Literary History*, New Delhi: Roli Books, 2003.

Evenson, N. *The Indian Metropolis, A View toward the West*, New Haven, London: Yale University Press, 1989.

Fergusson, J. *History of Indian and Eastern Architecture*, New Delhi: Munshiram Manoharlal, 1876.

Ganguly, K.M. 'A brief history of Andul Raj', 1 January 1900.

Gupta, B.K. *Sirajuddaulah and the East India Company, 1756-1757*, Leiden, 1962.

Gurner, C.W. *The Merchant Zamindars: Bengal Past and Present*, 1925.

Hunter, W. *The Annals of Rural Bengal*, Sixth ed. 1883; Calcutta: Indian Studies Past and Present, 1965.

Lang, J. *Architecture and Independence, the Search for Identity: India 1880 to 1980*, UK: Oxford University Press, 1997.

Losty, J.P. *Calcutta: City of Palaces, a Survey of the City in the Days of the East India Company, 1690-1858*, London: Arnold Publishing, 1990.

Majumdar, (née Bonnerjee) J.A.P. *Family History*, Delhi: Oxford University Press, 2003.

Marshall, P.J. 'The White Town of Calcutta under the rule of the East India Company,' in *Modern Asian Studies*, 34, 2, 2000.

Metcalf, T.R. *Forging the Raj, Essays of British India in the Heyday of the Empire*, New Delhi: Oxford University Press, 2005.

Mitter, P. *Art and Nationalism in Colonial India*, 1850-1922, *Occidental Orientations*, Cambridge: Cambridge University Press, 1994.

Muckherjee, S.N. 'A city of splendid palaces and dingy streets: Fiction as History', Seventh A.L. Basham Lecture delivered under the auspices of the Faculty of Asian Studies at the Australian National University, Faculty of Asian Studies, the Australian National University, 1987.

Mukhopadhyay, B. *Fading Glories of Monarchism*, Calcutta, 1988.

Nair, P.T. *A History of Calcutta's Streets*, Calcutta: Firma K.L. Mukhopadhyay, 1987.

Palit, C. *Tensions in Bengal Rural Society, Landlords, Planters and Colonial Rule 1830-1860*, Hyderabad: Orient Longman, 1998.

Pannikar, K.N. *Culture, Ideology, Hegemony, Intellectuals and Social Consciousness in Colonial India*, London: Anthem Press, 1995.

Roy, S. *Calcutta: Society and Change: 1690-1990*, Rupa and Co., 1991.

Salahuddin, A.F. *Social Ideas and Social Change in Bengal, 1818-1835*, Leiden, 1965.

Sinha, N.K. *The History of Bengal, (1757-1905)*, Calcutta: University of Calcutta, 1967.

Sinha, P. *Nineteenth-century Bengal, Aspects of Social History*, Calcutta: Firma K.L. Mukhopadhyay, 1965.

Tadgell, *The History of Architecture in Indian Architecture, from the Dawn of Civilisation to the End of the Raj*, London: Design and Technology Press, 1990.

Tillotson, G.H.R. *Paradigms of Indian Architecture*, Britain: Curzon Press, 1998.

Thomas, P. *Hindu Religion, Customs and Manners*, Bombay: Taraporevala Sons, 1975.

Acknowledgements

My parents, Alexander and Joan Herron, my husband Bryan and son Nicholas Taylor. With special thanks to INTACH (Indian National Trust for Art and Cultural Heritage) Calcutta Regional Chapter for graciously and unconditionally supporting my work in Calcutta.

Madhu and Saroj Nathany
G.M. Kapur
Sandip and Shruti Poddar
Amit and Aarti Nathany
Nandita Palchoudhuri
Udbhav and Vidisha Poddar
Amit and Sonali Basu
Deepak Bhandari
Princess Karuna Devi
Partho Ghose
Pradeep and Sarvani Guptoo
Aloke Laha
Akhil Sarkar
Anindyo Karforma
Pradeep Kumar Mitra
Rajdeep Ghosh
Ashutosh and Mitali Laha
Dibyendu Law
Kamal Basu
Subodh Bose
Milon Datta
Raja Mookerjee
Kari Mullick
Hirendro and Suven Mullick
Professor S.N. Mukherjee
Esha Bhattacharjee
Pabitra Das
Kalyan Deb
Probal Deb
Sandeep Deb
Debashis Nayak
Dr Chittaranjan Panda
Professor Samir Rakshit
Gautam Roy
Mrs Kalpana Roy
Professor Barun De
Samarendra Roy
Aranya Sen
Gour Shaw
Anmol Vellani
Biswas Family
Anup Saha
Kanak Roy
Maharam Kaliyar Dal Dev
Professor Jon Lang
Amanda Louth
Judit Korner
Lynn Sutherland

Index

A

B

C